Grandmother Earth Publications:

Ashes to Oaks
Grandmother Earth's Healthy and Wise Cookbook
Kinship
Living His Dream: A Farm Journal by a City Slicker
Of Butterflies and Unicorns
Take Time to Laugh: Its the Music of the Soul
To Love a Whale
View from a Mississippi River Cotton Sack

Cover Photo: Spring, Great Swamp,
Morris County, N. J. by C. Hogenbirk.

GRANDMOTHER EARTH I
1995

GRANDMOTHER EARTH I
1995

FEATURING AWARD WINNING POEMS

Edited by
Frances Brinkley Cowden
Marcelle Brinkley Zarshenas

Cover by Cornelius Hogenbirk

GRANDMOTHER EARTH CREATIONS

ISBN 1-884289-09-6   14.95

FIRST EDITION: 1995--PEERLESS PRINTING

GRANDMOTHER EARTH CREATIONS
8463 Deerfield Lane
Germantown, Tennessee 38138

DEDICATED
to the memory of

Our concept of Grandmother Earth is expressed by these lines from one of the prize-winning poems. The earth is our home, not a creating deity in itself.

> "We hopefully will stop to consider
> All the blessings we've had since birth;
> One of the greatest God has provided
> Is our home--Grandmother Earth."

--Embree Bolton

GRANDMOTHER EARTH CREATIONS prints all books on recycled paper in accordance with their philosophy of helping to preserve the earth. For the same reason most of the customary blank pages are omitted.

CONTENTS

FIRST ANNUAL AWARD WINNERS

I. **Beauty of Nature or Environmental Issues**
    First: Kristin P. Morrill, Mendon, MA
"Earth's Extinction"...12
    Second: Embree Bolton, Cordova,TN
"Images" 22
    Third: George V. Mylton, Boise, ID
"Terra Extremis"...100
    Fourth: Joan Anson-Weber, Roswell, GA
"City Flora" 26

II. **Man's Relationship to Man: In Memory of Donald Cowden who was killed by a Drunk Driver.**
    First: Malra Treece, Memphis TN
"On the Walls at Weidman's"..............................13
    Second: Adeline Lynn-Allyn, San Luis Obispo, CA; "Native Preserves"...............................28
    Third: Susan L. Rae, Loveland CO
"Love Dancing"...40
Fourth: Rosemary Stephens, Memphis, TN
"The Vigil" 56

III. **Poet's Choice**
    First: Linda M. Kay, Cabot , AR;
"Heirloom" 18
    Second: William Holland. Memphis, TN
"Newspapered Walls"..42
    Third: Maureen Cannon, Ridgewood, NJ
"How He Died"
    Fourth: Rosemary Dolgner, Lynchburg, VA
"Bric a Brac"...27

HONORABLE MENTION

Malra Treece, Memphis, TN
Embree Bolton, Cordova, TN
Rosemary Stephens, Memphis, TN
D. Beecher Smith II (3), Memphis, TN 46
Harold Baldwin, Memphis, TN 49
Dallas D. Lassen (4), Fleetwood, NC 35
Frances Darby, Memphis, TN 29
Sandra L. Lassen (2), Fleetwood, NC 32
Verna Lee Hinegardner, Hot Springs, AR 20
Margot Marler (2), Rossville, GA 44
Lori C. Fraind, Reston, VA 25
W. S.. Riley, Roy, WA 59
John W. Crawford, Arkadelphia, AR 86
Diane M. Clark, Memphis, TN 79
M. D. Ross, Lake Tahoe, CA 52
Gina Larkin, Edison, NJ 38
Ray C. Davis, Mexico 91
Dan Henry, Stockton CA 40

POEMS BY CHAPBOOK WINNERS

WINNER: *ASHES TO OAKS*
Shirley Rounds Schirz
Fennimore, Wisconsin 66

HONORABLE MENTION:
Betty Lou Herbert, Coeur d'Alene, Idaho......21
Burnette B. Benedict, Knoxville, Tennessee....64
Pat Benjamin, Oak Ridge, TN......................60
Patricia Fritsche, Indianapolis, Indiana..........68
Barbara A. Rouillard
West Springfield, Massachusetts

1994 CONTEST JUDGES

Marcelle Brinkley Zarshenas
Elaine Nunnally Davis
Eve Braden Hatchett

OTHER CONTRIBUTORS

Cornelius Hogenbirk 11, 61, 69, 74
Babs Hajdusiewicz..............................41
Cappy Love Hanson.........................45
Sister Mary Ricarda McGuire.........47
Edith Guy..88
Lucile Byrd Pitchford......................31
Geraldine Crow.................................75
Martha McNatt.................................70
Rebecca Pierre.................................102
Vassar Smith......................................97
Gladys Johns Scaife 100
Marsha Joan Grant............................50
Eric Grove...51
Martha Calloway...............................90
Sarah Briar Kurtz 93
Elaine Nunnally Davis 80
Eve Braden Hatchett...............88, 104
Frances Brinkley Cowden..............106

Readers are invited to send poems to the
1995 Poetry Contest. For Rules see page 111.

Vanessa virginiensis, American Painted Lady on Zinnia
Photo by Cornelius Hogenbirk

EARTH'S EXTINCTION

Yesterday of long ago
Before my self became me
The forests sang
And birds spoke freely
The night was alive with moon-beams

Tomorrow of another day
After I've changed from me to eternity
The fallow ground
With choked, empty air above
Has infinite darkness beneath a shrouded sun

With floating fish on oily seas
And mountains parched bald in the sun
This spinning orb, in cloud of ash
Spins on...with our children enraged
Powerless as tumble-weed in Oz.

--Kristin P. Morrill
Mendon, Massachusetts

ON THE WALLS AT WEIDMAN'S

Weidman's restaurant in Meridian, Mississippi,
since eighteen hundred seventy,
is thought to be forever.

The head of a young deer, over the fireplace,
has looked down on generations of diners.
The deer would have been dead now of old age
even if somebody hadn't shot it.
Its fine antlers, poised for flight,
would have been broken and rotted away.

A navy lieutenant, a major in the Marines,
sailors in white caps, sergeants, privates,
all smiling with young eyes and white teeth
into a future that turned out to be an eternity.

Notice that group of older men at the table,
drinking coffee. They escaped.

But nobody on the wall is bald or stooped
or big around the middle or has shaking hands
or stares into space with tired eyes.

Like the graceful deer
the strong men on the wall
remain young forever
behind protective glass

in shining gold frames
to match their stars
on the walls at Weidman's.

--Malra Treece

HOMECOMING, CONTINUED

We cannot lose those places
where we loved,
especially the first ones.

They cling like bits of fog
and return again and again in dreams
slanted or exact.
We hasten up worn steps
to greet those long gone
who routinely go about
the daily chores of living.

We have been told that we can't go home again
that things have changed and so have we
but the most important consideration
is that we never managed to get away.
We grasp backward
yearning for unity

for the closing of the circle
for the gathering together
of our scattered selves.

Thus, occasionally,
we return our tired bodies,
our automobiles, families,
accomplishments,
and old dreams
to a place
hard to find
on a map.

--Malra Treece

From: *Voices International*

SAIDA

I am Saida, a Phoenician of Carthage.
My first-born son is named Hannibal,
but I call him Son. My son,
although his father named him.
There are many Hannibals in Carthage
because the name means "Favored by Baal."
No one is favored by Baal Hammon.

Son is tall and brown as an olive seed.
His teeth are as white
as the tips of the waves of the sea.
He dives for fish and brings them to me,
his shining eyes the color of love.

Baal Hammon wants my son, the priests say,
as he has taken many.

His father says that we should buy a child,
from poor parents, to take his place at
the altar to Baal. This is done.
They are sold like sheep to be strangled,
their little bodies burned.
Thousands of little burnt bones
are stored in urns under stone markers,
bones and markers that have accumulated
for centuries.
They say this has always been the custom.

I could never sacrifice another mother's child.

Anyway, Baal is more pleased with the
offering of one's own,
especially the first-born son.

My husband and neighbors believe
that Baal must be pacified
so that the grain will grow
so that the olive trees and fig trees will bear fruit
so that the fish will be plentiful
so that life will be long

and women will be fertile
to produce more children for Baal Hammon.

I say to my husband,
"What could Baal possibly do to us
that would be worse than his taking Son?"
My husband says that all the other children
could die.

Not one person has ever seen Baal,
I hate him, whether or not he exists.

Our land is rich and beautiful,
but I hear that not too far away
there is a burning desert
with only occasional water and little food.
Son and I shall go there,
slipping away in the darkness.

I pack canteens of water, as much as we can carry.
I pack cheese, bread, figs, dates, olives, nuts,
dried fish, and more water.
Fishhooks, just in case.
Son's bow and arrow.
Blankets and extra sandals. More water.

Baal Hammon shall not have my Son.

--Malra Treece
Memphis, Tennessee

HEIRLOOM

The lines of a poem, visually
a curtain, a wind-blown finished end,
seam-sewn, and dipped in the madder dye
        of living roots,
can hold memory
like the black persistence of a fly,
or a whole shaky fleet of
long-legged mosquitoes,
here a poke, there a pinch,
or they can tear away completely,
trying to hold a wave
as a fishnet tries to hold the ocean,
and catches more, this silvered filigree,
these red hearts.
The lines of a poem can be a veil: are those
laughing eyes behind it?
Are those the eyes of the long-dead
        grandmother slicing rutabagas, laughing
until she cried, and the ceiling onion-hung?
Are those the threads of her braided hair,
woven to be a dream-catcher?
Are those the wooden slats, the shutters closed,
of quiet, death-watch days?
The lines of a poem,
like a black dress, can hide too much,
or they can be so ragged, the eye sinks
        to white bone.

                                --Linda Kay

THE WEANING OF ELVIRA

At the white board fence,
Whose whiteness is all up front,
towards the road, the company side,
from where visitors cannot see
the backside lift mossy and green,
there stands our little green cow
bawling for her bottle, bursting
as though all her fibers were hurting,
her harp of ribs played and played
by imaginary waves of hunger--she is so spoiled
and wants her mother, who is me,
both wishing for an udder and silence
and all day to walk together
around the small field
one man cleared by hand to raise
fescue for us among the stumps.
If I stood on four double toes,
I would gallop this heaven of brilliant green;
I would fatten sweetly and quietly,
tasting and tasting and growing huge on love.

                              --Linda Kay
                              Cabot, Arkansas

SONG FOR THE UNBORN

Sing a song for unborn babies, murdered
  millions every year, who had no choice,
  no chance to touch a mother's cheek
  or clutch a father's finger;

Sing for the miserable mothers and fathers
  no matter the age, no matter the
  reason, who cannot bear burdens;

Sing for parents and grandparents suffering
  daylight questioning and midnight
  terror worried about shame
  while colluding in murder;

Sing for unwanted things, unfinished things,
  uncelebrated birthdays,
  undelivered diplomas;

Sing for frightened fetuses, fleeing
  from needles, and needing
  only a little more time to be;

Sing for nurses and physicians who closet
  consciences, black out blood and flush
  throbbing body parts;

Sing for hospitals, clinics and abortion
  centers harboring endings
  of beginnings;

Sing for congressmen, senators and the president
  who have the right to govern the
  plight of an unborn baby;

Sing for the world
    prolonging life in near-lifeless forms
    while terminating life in unborn forms.

Sing -- if you can.

                    --Verna Lee Hinegardner
                      Poet Laureate of Arkansas
                      Hot Springs, Arkansas

FROSTING

The frost upon my windowpane,
Enchants me with its scene.
The fronds of fern and flowers grow,
In crystal, white, pristine.
A fairyland all made of ice,
So beautiful to see.
Where Titania reigns supreme,
And sparkles back at me.
But even as I watch, the sun
Strikes fire from the glass,
and all this magic artistry,
Begins to melt and pass.

        --Betty Lou Herbert
          Coeur D Alene, Idaho

IMAGES

The sun snuggled safely
behind the multi-colored cloud
as it quietly crept away.

The sun winked quickly
through the pines
as it darted out of sight.

Layers of clouds rolled back
like a blanket
to warm the sky
from the wintry breeze.

Columns of stone
chiseled away by wind and rain
formed bookends
for the trees wedged between.

Like a withered hand
the branches of the dead oak tree
clasped the fog
on the gentle hillside.

Unsalted tears gently bathed
the velveteen petals of the rose
tucked among the thorns.

The hues of the covenant
softly stroked the sky
burdened by clouds.

Tiny waves nibbled at a sand castle
before taking one huge bite
and darting quickly back
to the safety of the ocean.

--Embree Bolton

GRANDMOTHER EARTH'S BIRTHDAY

Grandmother Earth had a birthday party,
And all of nature came
To celebrate this great occasion
To honor her wonderful name.

The lion, the tiger, the bear, and the ox,
Giraffes and deer and elephants, too--
The bee, the goose and the sly old fox
Had been invited to attend the "do."

"How old is she?" asked the sparrow,
As a hush swept o'er the land;
Nothing was stirring anywhere,
Not even a speck of sand.

The silence was finally broken
By the darling kookaburra's laugh,
"Grandmother Earth's not sensitive to age,
As long as you cut it in half."

"She's older than us," said the monkeys.
"And all of us," cried the sheep.
"And us," said the sun, the moon and the stars.
"And us," said the fish from the deep.

Father Time bellowed out in a hurry,
In a voice with its deepest bass,
"Grandmother Earth's getting wrinkles
All over her ageless face."

As time has waited for no one
From now to eternity past,
"Let's live each day to protect her
So Grandmother Earth will last."

The birds and clouds all nodded,
The redwoods and pines bowed in prayer,
In hopes that all who live here
Will treat Grandmother Earth with care.

We hopefully will stop to consider
All the blessings we've had since birth;
One of the greatest God has provided
Is our home--Grandmother Earth.

--Embree Bolton
Memphis, Tennessee

THE WOLF'S SIDE OF THE STORY

"The truth is, Little Miss Red Ridinghood,
I am very much misunderstood.
I really mean your Granny and you no harm,
If it were my choice,
        I'd stay away from your farm.
But they built a highway through my habitat
In such a mindless way that I can't get at
The land I used to roam,
The land I called my home.
And the developments are encroaching,
and the local boys get their kicks by poaching.
Your fear of me has given me a bad name,
And for thousands, millions of hunters, made me
'fair' game.
Although it's hardly fair that
        they each have a gun,
And I have none.
I am a loner, I'd keep to myself
And have no intention of raiding
        Granny's cupboard shelf,
If I had a place to live--not rest--in peace
And not be maligned in children's stories as
        an evil beast."

                                    --Lori C. Fraind
                                    Reston, Virginia

CITY FLORA

What whimsical breeze lodged your seed
in this strange fissure
between dirt-encrusted slabs of paving
pulsating beneath a million steps?
What tenacity of nature inspired
your loveliness to blossom
in this steel land?
Opaline, your tiny thread of life
wished its way up towards
air-polluted streets,
catching a ray of sun, window-reflected
like a butterfly that enticed you lightly.
Imagine the bewilderment
on your astonished petals' floral memory
(innocently veined as a baby's temple)
to find yourself *sans* kith or kin
or mother's good earth!
Who has the depth of vision
to discover your niche,
and liberate you gently to outstretched fields
before your small fragrance
is crushed?

--Joan Anson-Weber
Roswell, Georgia

BRIC A BRAC

Cousin Lil died unexpectedly;
appeared on the streets of heaven
bewildered, carrying the little
silver tray that no one on earth
could ever find again. We used
to say "Lil took it" whenever
something was missing. A comfort
to think of her little nest up there
(yes, she finally settled down and
stopped asking the way home) with
all its loot, brushed or polished
faithfully as always. And chiefest
among these not-lost treasures:
the silver tray, reflecting a thin
sweet face that grows wispier in
the light of the sun of suns.

--Rosemary Dolgner
Lynchburg, Virginia

NATIVE PRESERVES

I moved from place to place
before my birth
in cells of people I never knew
but heard of later on
became familiar with as time
      went by.
I came from Sweden in a shaft
of hair--from the Big Horn
in Lakota bones, and cells
came dancing in a leprechaun's
smile; a smile I used when
I was young and my father drank
and food was gone.

I bore my sons from place
to place in cells from people
they never knew
but heard of later on
became familiar with as time
      went by.
Out of English mists, a sense
of style; from prairie sod
in firm square jaws
and cells came dancing in a
leprechaun's smile--used
by my sons when they were young
and surfing strong.

My sons carried children who
carried their own from place to

place in cells from people they
never knew, but will hear of
later on, become familiar with
         as time goes by.
From Spain, expressed in lean
brown hands; in vocal cords
from northern climes, and some
cells ride in a Navajo's heart;
while others still dance in a
leprechaun's smile used by these
children while they are young.
                    --Adeline Lynn-Allyn
                 San Luis Obispo, California

REFRESHINGLY AUTUMN

There is about the land a sense of urgency
Lawn grasses only inches high bear heads
            heavy with seed
Summer blossoms reduced in size now seemingly
         more brilliant in color.
Edges of leaves are tinged with oranges,
            reds and yellows
Erasing quickly the lush green of the summer.

Insects scurry into secret mounds

or earth's deep recesses
To rest from their noisy resounding
din of summer nights.
No longer does the squirrel playfully
shake the dogwood branches
To munch on plentiful ripened red berries;
Tell-tale patches in the lawn appear to conceal
Fruits earlier stored for future use.
Outer hulls of a pecan lie in the open driveway
Plucked underripe from the tree, its bitter
contents consumed or buried deep.

A distant sound prompts an upward glance
To view the V-shape formation of wild geese;
With luck their raucous honking can be heard
Above the loud and steady drone
of high-flying jet planes
That leave widening white streaks across the sky.

Soft, warm playful winds that
caressed the summer
Sweep more strongly into a forceful push
To snatch freshly loosened leaves from baring
branches.
Furry coats on house pets fluff and thicken
Cats become kittenish, dogs playful pups.
Morning sun rays slant more
from east and north
To cast shadows now from south and west.
Evening sun sets to redden skies earlier
Drawing to a chilly close the autumn day.

Man picks up the increasing pace

On steady sound of rushing feet.
Respite comes from lingering heat of summer
As changes awaken a stirring from within.
Thoughts now retreat to seek and center
On soulful peace.

--Frances Darby
Memphis, Tennessee

GENTLEMAN OF PROMISE

Dedicated to the memory of Fred Snover, a talented poet with a great sense of humor.

He took my hand in warm, firm grasp,
cradled it gently in both his,
looked deep into my eyes
and assured me my future would be safe with
 him.
He spoke of his concern for me
        and how it would be his priority.
I knew the QUESTION was coming.
I was ready with my answer.

How could anyone refuse
this dynamic, charismatic man?

He put his arm around my shoulders.
"Tomorrow," he said, "Tomorrow is crucial.
May I count on your vote?"

--Lucile Byrd Pitchford
Memphis, Tennessee

Sandra and Dallas Lassen teach creative writing and genealogy.
During their six years of marriage, they have only been apart one day.
They work side by side on "dueling computers."

WHO OWNS MOUNTAINS?

Who owns mountains?

Oh, I know the power company holds
the right of way
where foxes play, where the cut is in the tree line
and those monster poles slice the forest
pole legs spread like metal mountain men
but who owns mountains?

Through miles of easy curves
sunlight chases shade in trees along the ridge.
The robin visits here, but does not stay.
She has her route laid out from north to south.
The deer, also, is tenant here.

When first the mountains melted down
and cooled
and hardened once again to rocky crust,
who owned them then?
Indians passed this way, cut foot trails, hunted
took little with them when they left
and never sought to own the mountains.

We make too much of ownership.

In winter once, I had a cat who came around
when he was hungry
or when he was cold. He used my lap
for sleeping.
I used his coarse, black fur for stroking
by the winter fire.
In spring, he went away without
a backward glance.
We understood we did not own each other.

Maybe no one owns the mountains.

And if you think that tall pine
on the western slope
points his accusatory finger
it just might be
like the pine, the robin, and the deer
we are only tenants here.

No one, I think, owns mountains.

--Sandra Lake Lassen

THREADS

The last two females of our line, we pack
our mother's half-sewn quilt away.

My sister stitches that same way
with rows of basting carefully wrought
while I, the keeper of the family tales
receive old letters, photographs
recall our mother's telling
of starving times, of cholera and mountain men
feuds, courtships, burials.
She wove with words
the fabric of our family.

We pack and wonder
who will learn the stitches
from my sister's steady hand
or hear our women's stories told.
Sons, brothers, nephews, marry
breed more sons, separate, divorce
and we fragment
like ragged patches on a crazy quilt
in the basket
next to mother's favorite chair.

--Sandra Lake Lassen
Fleetwood, North Carolina

OUT ON A LIMB
(Acid Rain)

LISTEN
TO THE
TREES
TODAY,
tomorrow
may be too
late. Nature's
leaves are gone in May.
This blight kills along the way.
LISTEN TO THE TREES TODAY.
Towers belch the acid spray.
Colors change with no rebate. Nature's
leaves are gone in May. It makes eyes sting
every day. Think about it, concentrate, LISTEN
TO THE TREES TODAY. Rain doesn't wash it away,
it carries pollutants state to state. Nature's leaves are
gone in May. For this tragedy we will pay. To this
problem
we all relate.
LISTEN
TO THE
TREES
TODAY

--Dallas D. Lassen

DOWN AND OUT
(Villanelle)

Hey mister! Got a fin?
Down on my luck, lately, man.
Just need a little to start again.

I'm cold and hungry, that's a sin.
I need a few bucks, got a plan.
Hey, mister! Got a fin?

You gotta' put somethin' in the tin
so I can eat, that's why I pan.
Just need a little to start again.

Don't leave me sir, got no kin,
I need some help from you my man.
Hey, mister! Got a fin?

Had a job, was on the mend
then took a drink, was in the can.
Just need a little to start again.

Hey, man! I need a friend.
Bottle's empty, dry as sand.
Hey mister! Got a fin?
Just need a little to start again.

--Dallas D. Lassen

FORKED TONGUE HERITAGE

Smoke puffs in clouds talked
to warriors with aces
bows and arrows.
Pioneers with muskets
on wagon trains,
Indian wars of yesteryear,
terror on the western plains.

Smoke puffs in clouds,
diesels or smokestacks,
intruders called this progress.
Warriors with women and children,
now on reservations,
no weapons, no communication, no job.
They escape with Jack Daniels
to deaden the sorrows of today
with little hope for tomorrow.

--Dallas D. Lassen

SUMMIT UP

Mountain ranges, playgrounds,
beaver feeding in the valleys,
grizzlies foraging in snow,
stately pines,

crisp, clear, clean air,
beauty forever?

Sounds of saws,
monsters belching smoke,
logs on the move,
clean air, now fumes.
The stage is still there,
but the players are gone.

--Dallas D. Lassen
Fleetwood, North Carolina

HARASS

Words spoken in the office.
Words, only words.
What harm?
Words, only words.
He speaks of large parts.
I feel small.
He speaks of wanting.
I feel dirty.
Small.
What did I say? Do? Wear? Not wear?
Dirty.

Scared child.
Did I hear
Scared
What I heard?
Small.
Dirty.
Where to go?
Who to tell?
Scared.
Hide.
Small.
Dirty.
All the self-defense courses
And women's "lib"
Cannot prepare me for the words,
Words.
Only words.
What harm?
Small.
Dirty.
Scared.
Hide from the words.
Hide the words.
Small.
Dirty.
Hide.
Don't scream.
Hide. Hide. Hide.

--Gina Larkin
Edison, New Jersey

LOVE DANCING

I'm dancing the love waltz
Down a winding, endless path,
I started out so blindly
And there's no turning back.

I'm two-stepping over mountains
Forging passes where I can
The elements are raging
So I dance as best I can.

I rumba to the beat of hearts
And *do-si-do* through strife
There's only one dance with you,
The ballet of my life.

I gaze into the depths
Of my leading man's sweet eyes
Reflected is my destiny
Love dancing, you and I.

--Susan L. Rae
Loveland, Colorado

SONG OF THE CROW

The crows in the palm trees
Screaming their song
Calling like battle-cries
Rise from the branches.
Black jagged wings
Beat at the air
Like dark fans.
Scavengers searching
For sustenance,
For life in bits and pieces.
Cleaning up
After someone else's leavings,
Nature's janitors.
Plumage shines and flashes
Like living night.
A lone crow hops.
Cocks its head,
Picks up a crumb
And takes to the air.
The voice of the crow scratches,
His song is his flight.

                              --Dan Henry
                         Stockton, California

NEWSPAPERED WALLS

Newspapers dulled the winds
and taught us names and places
on the walls where supper cooked
and daddy slept his dreams away--
our golden dreams in print
like books so rare so tattered at our school.
Big word headlines read at night
across the shimmering room
through the yellow kerosene.
The color clung we thought
and turned the papers yellow too.
We peeled the layers back
and read about mysterious things,
Wall Street, gunboats on the Yantzee River,
of Roosevelt, New Deal, Day of Infamy,
of Miss Martha Wilson's marriage
in a formal garden rite,
hamburger 15 cents a pound at Habeeb's,
and saw the flickering eyes of old man Allen
dead these twenty years.
Momma boxed our ears when we pulled the
layers back,
but back we pulled, five, six, sometimes eight
layers in a row.
They kept us warm and reading
when all light of hope seemed gone,
and I still can smell the kerosene
that lighted my first steps in knowing.

                              --W. H. Holland, Jr.

THE F-15

It flew
because
aerodynamically
that's what it's designed
to do,

but,
consider the bumble bee,
poor thing,
ill-designed,
obviously incapable of flight,

yet,
try to convince
the blossom on the apple tree
or the honeysuckle's tube
that this is so,

or the hive
renascent
through flights
of honied legs.

Curious
that much of nature
cannot understand
the laws of man.

--W. H. Holland, Jr.
Memphis, Tennessee

EARTH EMINENCE
HAIKU SEQUENCE

An ever changing
color canvas of drama:
a wonder, the Earth.

Honeysuckles breathe
softly, fragrance into space:
silent miracle.

In the fine mist of
the foaming wall of water,
a rainbow appears.

On leaves and blossoms
the dew rests like diamonds
in the morning sun.

Butterflies flutter
like Ginkgo leaves in the wind:
golden-winged dream.

--Margot Marler

THE WALL,
WASHINGTON D. C.

Overfullness of soul,
guided by my heart,
I stood before the Wall.

Reflections echoed
regret and pain.
The names on black

too profound to measure.
GOD and I wept,
as we faced the Wall.

                    --Margot Marler
                    Rossville, Georgia

A MAGICAL REALISM
ECOLOGY POEM

Let's say the bullet misses this time, shatters
rock instead of rib. Let's say the pronghorn leaps
away, lives to love another day, and pronks in
celebration when his youngsters

sprout their horn buds.
And let's say that the coyote doesn't eat the
poisoned hawk who ate the poisoned mouse who
ate the poisoned grain. Just this once there's
some divine intercession--a hail storm, maybe--
lightning--
and she stays in her den, curled like a crescent
moon around her hungry puppies.

Let's imagine, just this once, that the duck
doesn't swallow the lead shot for his gullet, to
grind up corn and snails with, but picks
a pebble. And a branch falls on the trap and
springs it before the foxes flow like amber
tributaries down to the stream to drink.

Let's say that water still leaps to bright
freedom over beaver dams; that air still
explodes when a falcon swoops on a pigeon;
when an eagle hits a snow goose, and all
its feathers go incandescent.

Let's pretend it's all still
there, the sweetness, the antique violence.

Say we pin that photograph of Earth
From Space up on our walls. Sure, it's
risky. You get far enough away, and otters
gliding like sable sunlight down a snow
bank disappear. Valleys shrink. Even
mountains are only a string of snowy
pearls, and all those bands of old-

growth forest look like so much
destiny waiting to be manifested.

But in hope, let's say that someone takes a baby
condor, born at the L. A. Zoo, and holds her up
to the sky she was born to: an offering. Says her
name three times to stars: a manifesto. Say you
finally look down deep into the magpie's eye,
past amber and earth brown, into black, where
the whole soul of the planet and oblivion lie,
stretched out side by side, hand in talon.

--Cappy Love Hanson
Santa Fe,New Mexico

IF THE SHOE FITS...

We cannot blame the scientists. They did
    the best they could.
    They used their giftedness
    and we, if we are honest must confess,
    were quick with affirmation. We got rid
of heat in summer, and we made a bid

47

for throw-aways designed,
it seemed, to bless
those who thought leisure
would bring happiness.

If molecules escaped the lifted lid
of a Pandoric Box, who really cared?
Our scientists were trained and well prepared
to meet the unexpected, which they did!
They warned of ozone breakdown.
God forbid
that rejects from our atmosphere would get
so out of hand --
become so great a threat!

If harm was done by dangers of unforeseen,
some good would balance evil we believed.
Too late we learned pollution is obscene.
Too late we doubted progress we achieved.

Just yesterday we mocked the ozone threat.
We laughed because we were so unafraid.
We shunned the mores of our past, and yet
today we run from monsters we have made.

--Sister Mary Ricarda McGuire
Hot Springs, Arkansas

RAINBOW RAIN

Autumn's stage is still and bare,
no sound or movement anywhere;
Finally, a zephyr of a breeze
comes to whisper through the trees.

With all four seasons, any year's a bummer;
much of what survived a hot, dry summer.
Winter simply will not sustain,
so autumn honors with rainbow rain.

First a single brown leaf floats down;
soon a cascading kaleidoscope of color coats the
town;
golden yellow, burnt orange, and carmine red
combine to form nature's perfect boyhood bed.

These, with other hues from The Master's brush,
assure room for spring's early, new growth crush;
Each fall I relive my youth again,
courtesy the crackle and rustle of rainbow rain.

--Harold E. Baldwin
Memphis, Tennessee

From: *Tennessee Voices*

KINDNESS

It takes
Kindness to try to save
A
Whale
A beached whale is
Like a stranger in a strange
Land
A stranger wanders in
dark afraid
Dark is a scary
Terrifying place
It exists in
Our minds
We each must
Travel through the
Dark
Chased by our demons and
Dragons
Dragons are animals like
Whales
It takes
Kindness to try to save
A
Whale. . .

--Marsha Grant
Memphis, Tennessee

From: *To Love a Whale*, an anthology for children
forthcoming in 1995.

By Eric Grove Grove, from the Cover of *To Love a Whale*

THE PICTURE

Watercolor haze
became oil,
sharp, crisp,
defined.
A new world
here, the color of peace
is love, and
the color of hope
is brotherhood.

Darkness ebbs,
the light rules
supreme.
Colors of light
cascade
over us all.
Restoring, healing,
painting us as one,
together
forever.

--M. D. Ross

CONTINUUM

The earth was bare,
naked,
as the night,
nature bloomed,
clothed,
gave her life,
man arose,
changed,
built,
invented,
scarred the land,
polluted the sky,
choking nature,
she was gone.
The earth was bare.

--M. D. Ross
S. Lake Tahoe, California

MY LOVE IS JACK'S BEANSTALK

My love is Jack's beanstalk:
one speckled dumb-bartered seed
unheeded, carelessly dropped,
that roots in sand and leaps
overnight into the sky.
High-reaching, you climbed it.

When giant boots come after you,
when giant voices hoot you back
to this gargoyled world
and you chop down this beanstalk,
what is left will make a tree
large enough to shade us,
higher than those bushes
other people lie under,
wider than those cautiously tended
plants with carefully pruned branches
some people still call love.

--Rosemary Stephens

From: *South and West*

MAID

Hattie is Watusi tall, reserved,
reaching without moving,
graceful as the wind -- even when
cleaning the bathroom bowl
she seems to be performing
ancient rites, on her knees
but still tall, looking down
on us somehow from
every household angle.

When she was a child she reached
upward in the cotton fields,
stretching for the cotton bolls
that later flew upward like
light into her hands,
making her palms shine.

For days after she has gone,
running smoothly to catch her bus,
we move sacrilegiously
in her cleanliness.

--Rosemary Stephens

From: *New Collage*

THE VIGIL

When they heard,
Her friends came,
Old women dressed in black,
And sat around her bed,
Iridescent grackles on a riverbank,
Watching for crocodile death.

The old women clicked their knitting needles
And clacked their tongues.
They remembered how she had laughed
And run, bright hair flying,
Through fields when she was young;
How she had walked beside
The man she married,
How she cried at his grave
Three children later.
And just two days ago
On all four graves, she placed
Bright flowers she had picked herself,
Stooping carefully, being no longer young;
Flowers she grew like those beside her bed
Which, even being cut,
Would now outlive her;
Flowers the color her hair used to be.

Wattles shaking, their rasping voices
Recalled her every deed and whim.
Their eyes glittered.

She would not bury them.
But even as they talked and waited,
They knew
Red-lit crocodile eyes
Watched from the depths of the river.

--Rosemary Stephens

From: *The Human Voice*

THE LITTLE MARES

The wind blows and the little mares
are skittish, for they know
why the wind blows,
who comes and why.
Run, little mares! Run
with manes uplifted,
run with high swishing tails!
Run with desperate eyes, red
nostrils wide, to hide
beneath chaste bending trees,
fending fretful on raped pastures! Run
from what the leaning grass portends!
But who can ever hide
from the lustful wind?

--Rosemary Stephens

From: *Poet*

WORKING MOTHER

The day begins where it ends,
morning forgotten. My
children yellow-jacket around
the room, my head buzzes,
life swarms, renewed by
my evening homecoming.

Fried eggs for supper (no meat at these prices!)
and cake I remembered, having forgotten it
yesterday
when smiles shook. Then I hold close each one
except the oldest, almost ten, whose hand
I touch, whispering my pride that she'll soon
be doing more than setting the table. I listen
to each one about important happenings of the
day;
I was not there, I could not share them until
now.
Each child is folded into bed, stamped
with a kiss and mailed to sleep.

I too sleep finally, fitfully, listening to boards
that creak beneath the weight of spirits,
all those ghosts who shall be always with us,
and that one ghost I saw tonight in the eyes,
the curve of cheek, the tone of voice, the gesture
of a hand so like, square-fingered.
The alarm sets off the ending;

breakfast and the leaving,
the setting aside of thoughts
except for uneasy concern
ringing far, far back in my head
till evening shakes itself
upon my hearth--and love
buzzes forth, alive and stinging.

--Rosemary Stephens
.Memphis, Tennessee

From: *Eve's Navel*, prize-winning chapbook published
by South and West.

INFINITE WALLS

Nature,
My home of high ceilings
And infinite walls,
Where my spirit wears
A dress of dreams
And nods,
Inebriated there
-- with God.

--W. S. Riley
Roy, Washington

YOUTH

We see
pink clover climb
the hills and touch the sky
with tiny fingers spread to grab
the sun.

--Pat Benjamin

"AND THEY WERE SORE AFRAID"

Timid, hunted creature ---
there you stand,
tilting your softly pointed ears
to catch the footfalls,
merging with the trees
you stand beside
like some tree spirit
slim and brown
that only flees
its sheltering bark
when all around
is motionless
and dark.
Why should we pity you,

as a creature strange --- apart?
We too stand frozen,
afraid to safely graze
on spring-green leaves
through warm, sun-dappled
days, afraid to turn
this way or that,
fearing attack, entrapment,
hunger, and pain.

--Pat Benjamin

Photo by Cornelius Hogenbirk.

"FLORIDA CRACKER"

What is it pulls me back ---
    to long white sandy roads,
        incandescent filaments
           shimmering,
        sealed in
by angular, tall pines ---
    scorching barefoot toes ---?

Heavy, the heat hovers
    through honey-suckled hours,
        sweetening shaded squalor
           of rotting
        cabin porches:

And only the gentle rustle
    of old newspaper fans
        or the drowsy cluck of hens
        disturbs
        suspended air,
    still motionless in time ---
        just as it was.

Rickety wooden rockers
    creak
        and sigh.

           --Pat Benjamin
            Oak Ridge, Tennessee

REVERENTIAL TOAST

Into this crystal night
Faceted with stars,
The new moon spills
Honeysuckle perfume,
A splash of dew,
And two moonbeams
To whisk in the pungent
Smell of pine and moist,
Deeply furrowed soil
Swirling northeastward
On the southwest wind--
My nostrils fill with this heady mixture,
Brewed and stored
Somewhere in Time's vast cellar;
On this occasion
With this rare vintage,
A reverential toast
I, kneeling with thanksgiving, make:
All praise and honor be to God
For His love through Christ His Son,
And all things beautiful and good...

--Burnette Bolin Benedict

DAY OF THE DRAGON

Oh where to survive can the wild geese go?
Tossed like shipwrecked waifs upon the tide,
With frantic cries they paddle to and fro.

Along the river bank wild roses grow,
For goslings, a blanket cozy they provide,
Oh where to survive can the wild geese go?
Steel teeth and claws no mercy know
Nor spare a single nest where goslings hide,
With frantic cries they paddle to and fro.

Daily grind the grim machines below
Sod, roots and rocks--all claims to home
denied--
Oh where to survive can the wild geese go?

Yellow dragons spitting smoke and woe
With roars chase nestling goslings far and
wide,
with frantic cries they paddle to and fro.
No sunsets on mossy bank and goslings glow--

Desolate gapes its grave where their habitat
died;
Oh where to survive can the wild geese go?
With frantic cries they paddle to and fro...

                    --Burnette Bolin Benedict

KINSHIP

A stately cedar once as I began,
A seedling reaching up to touch the sun,
Believing youthful sapling limbs could span
Celestial limits--cautious thoughts were none.
The pull of Earth and roots of home run deep,
And hearts of each are not immune to mark
Sparse years and ravages with scars, but keep
As talisman, each diurnal solar arc.
We share quiet mysteries of life which burn
Beyond our earthbound reach--to leave to fate
The grace required to bend or break we learn,
And hear of crowns whose prongs bright stars
  await.
Since Eden we have shared a common lot--
And lie stacked in Earth's final common plot...

--Burnette Bolin Benedict
Knoxville, Tennessee

These poems by Burnette Benedict are from her award-winning chapbook, *Kinship*, published by Grandmother Earth, January, 1995.

ASHES TO OAK

Stretch above me now.
with yet another purpose,
take me through your veins
to feed your new spring leaves
that breathe the breath of rain
and sun and grow and warm your soul
and mine.

Wrap around me with
your earthly mother arms,
cradle me and know
I am a pinnacle of life
for you, and you
for me and be that,
as long as
life itself may be.

--Shirley Rounds Schirz

WHEN I WRITE

When I write
I'm like a white-tipped eagle
that has soared countless flights,
many smooth, some too turbulent,
an aged eagle that glides easily
home on an old familiar course,
a soft, safe, eager, happy course.

That's the eagle's patterned way
and yours--and mine
no matter what our age
we soar and know
that we are free
once we know the way home,
and I am home when I write.

We have a home--
the eagle and his to find
and me and mine.

--Shirley Rounds Schirz
Fennimore, Wisconsin

These poems by Shirley Schirz are from her award-winning chapbook, *Ashes to Oaks*, published by Grandmother Earth, January, 1995.

DO WE CHOOSE OUR MEMORY TO BE BORN?

Does some incandescent lamp turn on
As we flip incessantly
Page after page
To find the right director.
Or our
Inner truth takes precedent.
Why this enchanted moment
needed so much attention.
A craving that the heart
Can turn and shake its head,
Could it have been a deeper love
Than all the dream
Of a midnight's choir in the
Joy discovered?
That in another time
The reality
Would be reminisced
In your choice
Of being. In this memoir.
The beginning of life.

--Patricia Fritsche
Indianapolis, Indiana

Skunk Cabbage unfolding, with young spathe yet to open,
Symplocarpus foetidus, (Mid-March).
Photo by Cornelius Hogenbirk.

BASIL
HERB OF ROMANCE

Martha McNatt

Perhaps the culinary herb used most widely in the United States is basil. In the South, the herb's name is often pronounced to rhyme with *hazel*, but most herb books confirm that it should rhyme with *dazzle*. Basil was first used in ancient India, where it was the object of much superstition, revered by some and scorned by others. It is often mentioned in the literature of ancient Rome and Greece.

One of the most interesting, if somewhat grisly, literary references to basil appears in a poem by the nineteenth-century English poet John Keats entitled "Isabella, or the Pot of Basil." Keats tells the story of a Florentine maiden who, when she discovers that her beloved Lorenzo has been treacherously murdered by her brothers, exhumes her dead lover's corpse and severs its head, putting it in a clay pot and planting sweet basil over it:

> *She had no knowledge when the day was done,*
> *And the new morn she saw not: but in peace*
> *Hung over her sweet Basil evermore.*
> *And moisten'd it with tears unto the core.*

Basil is an annual herb of the mint family. Many varieties exist; but in Tennessee garden stores, plants are usually labeled sweet basil, common basil, or garden basil. Plants may be started from seed indoors but should not be transplanted until all danger of frost is past, since basil is highly sensitive to cold temperatures. Here in Tennessee the herb may be grown by planting it in full sun, then thinning the plants to about twelve inches apart. I add compost and fertilizer to my basil bed each year in order to get lush foliage.

Harvesting of mature basil leaves should begin before the flowers appear but can be done several times during the growing season. I pinch off the flower shoots in order to prolong my plants' harvesting season. Leaves should be dried in the shade until they are crisp, then stored in a dark, dry place.

One formula for seasoning with basil is to use it in any dish containing tomatoes. I consider basil essential in soups, stews, pasta dishes and pizza. I add a handful of basil to the pot when I cook chicken, venison or pork. I also mix dried basil with thyme, parsley and hot peppers to make a season for blackened fish.

Recently, I had a dinner in a West Chicago Serbian restaurant, well known for its Eastern European cuisine. My hosts especially recommended the soup course. It was a rich vegetable mixture in a dark broth, heavily seasoned with fresh basil. Although the restaurant probably used lamb as a base, I used beef in developing my recipe, which pleases my family and tastes identical to the Chicago soup.

SERBIAN VEGETABLE SOUP

2 cups cooked beef chuck (mixed fat and lean)
2 cups rich beef stock
2 cups frozen mixed vegetables
1 large white potato (cubed, not peeled)
1 large onion, chopped
1 rib celery, chopped
2 cups canned tomatoes
1 large clove garlic, pressed
Fresh ground black pepper and salt, as desired.

Simmer in large saucepan until vegetables are tender. Add water as necessary if soup becomes too thick.
Serves 6.

IT'S A GOURD! IT'S A SQUASH! IT'S A DISHCLOTH! LOOFAHS!

Martha McNatt

The package was labeled "silly seeds." It was on a clearance table at the end of gardening season in a Memphis seed store. I kept the seeds in the freezer all winter and planted them along the garden fence in early May.

On the back of the package, the plant was identified as "loofah" and was described a natural sponge. I had seen them in bath specialty shops, advertised for removing dead skin from elbows and knees. Years ago, my mother received one from a friend, who called it a "dishrag gourd."

After I planted the seeds, almost overnight the garden fence was heavy with climbing vines and deep green leaves, irregularly triangular in shape. By the end of June, brilliant yellow flowers appeared, followed by little green fruits, shaped like a cucumber but vertically ridged and tapered on both ends. Little fruits quickly became giant ones, hanging thick along the fence, some resting on the ground and some meandering into the neighboring raspberry vines.

The package said the fruits were edible when young and tender, prepared in the same manner as zucchini or other summer squash. Since other squash were plentiful, I allowed all the loofah to pass the edible stage, which it did by the dozens.

What a weird plant! Is it squash? Actually, it is neither. *The New Illustrated Encyclopedia of Gardening* classifies it as a vegetable sponge, a member of the cucumber family. Its botanical name is *luffa*. Loofah grows wild in India and other tropical countries. It is sensitive to cold and grows best here when planted in warm moist soil.

By autumn in my garden, the picnic table was covered with mature loofah, the skins dark brown, brittle and easy to peel away, leaving giant cucumber shapes firm, dry and ready to carve into multiple forms. The shapes varied in color from tan to alabaster to almost white. Cutting it with a sharp knife was like cutting into styrofoam used for insulation or for mounting floral arrangements.

The cutting was fun. Inside were tunnels filled with black seed, which were easy to shake out. The tunnels were not all the same size, but generally, each loofah had four rows of seeds. A crosswise slice had four-leaf clover-shaped holes in the center.

A slab off the side became a bath sponge. Halved vertically a small loofah turned into a decorator soup holder. For a ladies' luncheon, cross-wise slices topped with red plaid bows were place favors. a basket full of various shapes decorated the hearth. A chunk at the kitchen sink is great for preparing dishes for the dishwasher. Everybody on my gift list received one for Christmas.

If I grow loofah again, I will have to change its location. My husband had a terrible time removing the remains of the vines from the garden fence. The earlier-mentioned garden encyclopedia says each plant will grow to a height of 10 to 15 feet, climbing by putting out tendrils.

The beauty of the foliage and the blossoms suggest loofah would be an excellent choice for a garden trellis. Has anyone tried that method? I would like to hear other gardeners' experiences with this unusual plant.

Articles by Martha McNatt, Jackson, Tennessee, have appeared in *The Tennessee Conservationist*. Author of *Feeding the Flock: The Cookbook for a Score or More*, she is featured in the forthcoming *Grandmother Earth's Healthy and Wise Cookbook* (March, 1995).

MOCKING BIRD

Listen to the mocking bird,
that many-tongued mimic,
clown-bird of song and gossip,
who will sing sweet and lovely
in the softness of a June evening
to lullaby the sun to bed.

Perched on my television antennae
--no mention of mocking bird
in my *TV Guide*--
after a rollicking outpouring of song,
mocking bird sans benefit of costume change
turns to its clown-bird act.

It mimics the sounds
of mate-seeking frogs
barks of dogs--shrills of cats
in neighborhood backyards.
The night serenades of cicada and cricket,
the creaking of my garden gate
after latching it shut
to close up for the day.

Pleasant dreams, mocking bird.
Tomorrow I'll be waiting here--
same place, same time
to listen to the mocking bird.

--Cornelius Hogenbirk
Waretown, New Jersey

THE RETURN OF THE BLUEBIRDS

Geraldine K. Crow

Four years without a family of bluebirds nesting in my yard! Now that's too long! I did what any good, bluebird-loving Christian would do. I prayed.

Five long years ago Betty and Bob Blue first occupied the birdhouse thirty feet from our bedroom window. Thy rent it for "a song." In April the bluebirds' soft, lyrical warbling was heard in the garden, around the pond and in the yard. High up in the leafless oak trees their courtship blossomed as the bright-blue male with burnt-orange breast and white belly offered the duller-colored female a caterpillar, and she fluttered her wings in gratitude. Earlier he had found the bird box in our yard; then he bought her to to inspect and approve it. In time she began constructing her neat cup-like nest with fine grasses and pine needles while he stood guard on a nearby jasmine vine trellis ready to fight off any intruders. Two weeks after she laid the last egg, five baby bluebirds emerged.

Mornings my husband and I awoke to the delicate, cheerful chatter of the Blues. Their sweet, animated sounds, having an almost human quality, seemed more live conversation than song. Many times during the day I went to the window for a glimpse of this handsome family-oriented pair who lifted my spirits with their presence.

Near summer's end only two young, blue-gray bluebirds with spotted breasts practiced their flying skills in the front yard and later splashed down in the birdbath. From nearby trees came the gentle sounds of their proud parents.

The following year I waited anxiously for the Blues to reclaim their home. One mid-April morning there stood Bob, erect and handsome, "riding shotgun" atop the trellis while a busy Betty searched for precisely the right pieces of nesting material.

The next afternoon my husband handed me the lifeless form of a female bluebird. Betty deceived by the reflection of the inviting woods mirrored in the bathroom window flew headlong into that peaceful sight to meet her death.

Shocked and saddened, I hurried to the bedroom window. There sat Bob on the trellis guarding the homestead unaware of his great loss. Fifteen minutes passed. Bob became restless. He flew from tree to tree searching for his mate. At dusk, Bob, forlorn, perched on the trellis turning his head in all directions apparently scanning the skies for a returning Betty.

The next day, 6:00 a. m. Bob looked inside the bird box. Alas! No Betty! He flew back to the trellis. Feathers fluffed, body slumped, head down, Bob kept his vigil in the chilling wind. Later that morning he disappeared. Around noon from the woods came the plaintive call of a bluebird.

"Bluebirds of happiness" leave a tremendous void when they are away for four years. Too many city dwellers have never seen a bluebird except in a poem, a song, or a greeting card.

Like the buffalo and the bald eagle, this native American bird, who also greeted the first colonists as they settled the east coast, has been badly mistreated. The Eastern Bluebird (*Sialia Sialis*), which inhabits the area east of the Rocky Mountains, is in jeopardy. It is estimated that during the past fifty years the blue bird population has declined ninety per cent.

As housing developments, freeways, shopping centers and parking lots encroached on the bluebird's territory, he escaped to a more peaceful, less crowded environment. He prefers open land surrounded by wooded areas, such as pastures, crop lands, rural roadways, orchards and gardens.

The bluebird's enemies and predators are many: sparrows, starlings, snakes, raccoons, pesticides, extremely cold winters and lack of food and nesting sites.

His choice of nesting sites is a hollowed-out cavity in a rotted tree or wooden fence post. Most wooden posts have been replaced by metal posts, and chain saws have quickly eliminated dead trees. fortunately, bluebirds really accept man-made birdhouses.

The bluebird is beneficial to man since his diet consists mainly of insects: caterpillars, cutworms and grasshoppers, and a small amount of fruit and berries, mostly wild berries. In the end of winter he can be seen dining on dried sumac berries. Most bluebirds in Arkansas stay in the vicinity where they breed except when driven further south by the cold weather and lack of food supplies.

Man is attempting to reverse the trend of the diminishing blue-bird population by setting up nesting boxes and bluebird trails. A bluebird trail consists of a series of nesting boxes placed more than 100 yards apart four to six feet off the ground. Karen Kohl, Urban Wildlife Biologist with the Arkansas Game and Fish Commission, is diligently working to boost the bluebird population in Arkansas through her Bluebird Trail Program. If you would like to become involved, order a packet of material about bluebirds from the Arkansas Game and Fish Commission, 2 Natural Resources Drive, Little Rock, Arkansas 72205. Study the material and the bluebird house plans.

If you do not have an area suitable for bluebirds, seek out an appropriate location for a bluebird box or a bluebird trail: a golf course, a park, a cemetery, a pasture, an orchard or garden (one where pesticides are not used). Ask permission from the owner to establish a bluebird trail on his property explaining what, why and how. Then promise to maintain and monitor the bird boxes throughout the year. Once owners become familiar with the program, they will gladly give you permission to do something they do not have time to do. Next build the boxes to specifications and set them in place.

Make a commitment by being responsible for at least one bluebird box this year. You will derive hours of pleasure observing the birds, and you will know the feeling of pride and accomplishment in helping a species survive.

Our own hard work--and prayers--have paid off. Our trail now reaches out to include three other farms near us. No, there isn't "a blue bird on my shoulder"--not yet. But the bluebirds have returned to our yard. This afternoon Bill and Becky Blue stood on the rock ledge outside my bedroom window, peered in, warbled tenderly to each other, then flew away. Beck is incubating five pale-blue eggs in the box thirty feet away.

From: *Living His Dream: A Farm Journal by a City Slicker,* Geraldine K. Crow's forthcoming book, Grandmother Earth, Spring, 1995.

DIVINE DESTINY

A pale orchid candle
　　Stands noble and tall,
　　　　Sending forth fragrant illumination
　　　　　To the four corners of the
　　　　shadowy room.
　　　　　　　Its fire rises boldly
　　　　　With steady authority,
　　Bending easily in the breeze,
　Then returning to its source.
The firm wax warms and melts,
　　Flowing gracefully and contentedly
　　　Into a new shape,
　　　　A different identity.
　　　　　　The candle gladly offers its gifts
　　　　　Of heat and golden light
　　　To the wide, welcoming walls
　　Of the empty room.
Consumed by its service,
　　It spends itself unselfishly
　　　　By burning in the holy flame
　　　　　And completing its destiny
　　　　　in darkness.

　　　　　　　　　--Diane M. Clark
　　　　　　　　　Memphis, Tennessee

Excerpts from *THE MOTHERS OF JESUS*, by Elaine Nunnally Davis, a commentary on the women listed in Matthew's genealogy, published by Life Press:

TAMAR

Tamar is the oldest mother mentioned in the genealogy of Jesus of Nazareth. She was the mother of twin sons Pharez and Zerah by Judah, son of Jacob. It was through Pharez, the firstborn, that the royal lineage passed. Because Judah was Tamar's father-in-law, the account is shocking to many Christians, but in the light of its own times and its own circumstances the events are much less so.

About the time Joseph was sold into Egypt, Judah left the social circle of the family. He went to stay with a man of Adullam and there married the daughter of Shua, a Canaanite. That marriage produced Er, Onan, and Shelah: three sons. At the proper time Judah took for Er a wife whose name was Tamar, but Er died without children. As was the custom in the culture, the next son married the widow to produce offspring for his brother. Following Onan's marriage to Tamar, he too died without leaving offspring. Judah, fearing some curse to be on Tamar and unwilling to give his only remaining son to her for fear that he too would die, told her to return to the home of her father and wait until Shelah was grown....

Tamar was, in effect, a perpetual widow.... Suddenly she had no husband and no child. Being childless in her culture was a severe reproach. Perpetuation of their lineage and security for their old age was of utmost importance in their lives. A woman was in disgrace if she did not bear a child....Tamar could not use the same method as her predecessors, for her situation was different from that of Sarah and Leah and Rachel. [They had allowed their husbands to have relations with their maids to produce a child for them.] Tamar's husbands had died. Without a husband, having a maidservant to give was irrelevant. Tamar's lack could not be solved by providing a maidservant for a surrogate mother. What she needed was a surrogate father.

Being childless was reproach enough, but that was not the full extent of her problems. Tamar had the reputation of being a curse. Two husbands had died rather soon after their marriages to her and there seemed to be no other plausible explanation. The fact that her father-in-law believed her to be the reason for their deaths merely confirmed it. And the fact that he acted on that belief by withholding Shelah from her gave great weight to the curse story in the community. There was, no doubt, a good deal of gossip and ridicule and ostracism in Tamar's life during those years. Her good name was now blighted through no fault of her own. Though the Lord had killed her husbands, no one knew that. The opinion leaders in the community had adjudged the victim to be the perpetrator and she suffered for it....

Tamar lived with her father. Why did he not come to her defense? There may have been many reasons. Wives were purchased for marriage by the family of the husband and she remained their property even though she resided in the home of her father. Perhaps her father had much less social standing than did Judah. Perhaps her father was ashamed. Perhaps he accepted Judah's assessment that she was a curse upon husbands. Perhaps he was so concerned with his business and his sons that the plight of his daughter was inconsequential to him. In truth, the culture placed little value upon pleasing women and Tamar's plight was not important to her father, nor to Judah, nor to

Shelah....

As Tamar waited, no doubt she talked with God and petitioned Him to vindicate her and to provide His blessings on her. And Tamar waited. In time, Shelah came of age. Still Tamar waited. A respectable time passed when it would have been appropriate to give her to Shelah. And Tamar continued to wait. The daughter of Shua died and Judah grieved. Tamar waited still. What if Judah, too, died? Where would be her hope then? Tamar's biological clock was winding down and she faced the very real possibility that she would be forever childless. Tamar waited no longer....

Tamar could have devised a plan to trick Shelah into fathering a child, but her rights did not rest with Shelah. She, like Shelah, was under Judah's authority even though she was residing in the household of her father. It was Judah who had instructed her to return to her father's household and she had obeyed....

Tamar waited no longer. The daughter of Shua had died and Judah was over his mourning. Hearing that Judah was on his way to Timnah to shear sheep, she exchanged her widow's clothes for other garments and covering her face with a veil sat in the entrance to Enaim. "When Judah saw her, he thought she was a prostitute, for she had covered her face."

He made arrangements with her, promising to send her a young goat. She asked for a pledge to assure that his promise of sending the kid would be honored. Her request was for his signet ring with its cord, and his staff. Judah complied. As a result of her transaction, the Lord gave Tamar conception by Judah which He had denied her by Er and Onan. When Judah left, she returned home and again put on her widow's garments.

When Judah sent the young goat back by his friend Hirah the Adullamite, the harlot could not be found and no man acknowledged that a prostitute had ever been there. Judah did not pursue the matter for fear of becoming a laughingstock among the men. He withdrew from the search and comforted himself in his honesty, for he had tried to pay the girl.

Was it by faith, Tamar changed her widow's clothes and covered herself with a veil and sat at the entrance to Enaim, knowing that Judah would be coming that way? Was she wicked? Was she seeking thrills, money, the pleasures of sex? Would she have transacted a relationship with a man other than Judah?

Religion in the land of the Canaanites consisted of a fertility cult. The religious services they participated in utilized prostitutes, both male and female. In their sexual activities, it was believed that they exercised a special worship of the fertility gods. Their lust and worship were intermingled and indulging in the one provided the virtue of the other. Not only that, but the evil in Canaan was approaching its peak. Had Tamar been lustful, she might have found a convenient way to be involved in the religious practices of the land and to be culturally absolved of any guilt for it. Tamar knew about these activities but was not a part of them, for she was not a Canaanite and she did not believe in their gods. The existence of the cult in the land, however, provided a plausible guise for the events that occurred.

That Tamar might be interested in lust and sexual pleasure in her duplicity with Judah introduces an element that is foreign to the account and obscures the true interpretation of a story of lineage. The Hebrews had a sense of urgency about family lines that is not popularly understood today. Tamar would not have made arrangements with another man, for no man outside the family could have accomplished the lineage which she sought. Judah was the nearest of kin to her husband, other than Shelah whom he had not directed to marry her. Judah was the one in charge of the situation and Judah's wife, now dead, was no longer a social or moral consideration with which Tamar had to deal. In light of the circumstances in which she found herself and the alternatives available to her, Judah was her correct choice to perpetuate the line of the oldest son.

As for wickedness, she had waited patiently for a long time. She had been wronged and deceived. It was Judah's responsibility to provide for the levirate marriage and he had chosen not to do so. Soon she would be past childbearing age. She would be childless and without promise. The motivations of Tamar and of Judah in the matter at Enaim are in direct contrast. He was looking for the pleasures of sex; she was looking for the pleasures of motherhood. His choice was a prostitute; hers was proper lineage.

As for money, Tamar received no pay for her sexual services to Judah. The goat was returned to the flock and the staff and signet and cord were returned to Judah after they had served their purpose. Her pay was what was due to her from the time she was betrothed to Er....

Three months later when Judah learned that his daughter-in-law was pregnant, he was indignant and called for the death penalty. There were no prohibitions against his sexual liaison, but women were under a different standard. It was his right to impose penalties for violations, for he was the head of the family and was responsible for the conduct of its members.... Tamar had known Judah well. She had known what he would do and what would happen. Two choices had been before her: The certainty of living death as a perpetual widow if she did nothing or the possibility of sure death as a prostitute if her plan failed. She had secured a ready defense for this moment and brought out the items she had required of him when he transacted with her before the gate at Enaim. They were the witnesses she needed to legitimize her transaction....

By the spirit, Tamar exerted her will and prevailed over Judah in a way that had tremendous consequences for the Israelite nation. God blessed her by giving her the seed of promise which culminated in Christ Jesus.

§§§§

RAIN

I want the rain.
Heavy, dark,
chasing-people-off-the-road,
dark-at-three-o'clock
rain,
the rain most people
say they hate.
(But that I think they secretly love.)
Sit-at-home-by-the window
Play-a-game-by-the-fire
Go-for-a-walk in the
rain.
I want the rain that shatters windows
Causes pile-ups
And knocks out power lines.
Rain.

--Linnea Hallmark
Seattle, Washington

I REMEMBER PAPA

My Papa was not a violent man.
He was very gentle-like the oft stroking
of a baby lamb's nose.
He was quiet and slow
like the moving of a turtle
on the new spring grass.

I remember him the most
for the stories he could tell
around hot stone fires
on a long winter's night --
tales of drunk Indians
he hid from in the dark
or tales of how his mother killed
the wild black panther
with a knot of hard red pine.

I remember him too for the fun he loved
      to make --
like hiding in the trees underneath a big sheet
or hitting on the boards of the old wooden floor
and screaming out aloud just to scare us
      young boys
on a bright spooky October night.

My Papa was a patient man.

But he could get real mad.
I remember so well when little Pue
came in about dark thirty one day

having spent several hours in the smoke-filled
        pool hall
leaving his wood unchopped and his hogs unfed.
Papa's patience then grew thin and he could
        not speak
for his tongue rolled round and round
getting caught between his teeth,
then turned red almost bleeding as he blurted
out his anger
with his hand slap on his trembling knee.
I remember that time in the dead of the winter
when he found missing the sweet cured ham
that had been seeping with the sugar
on the cold smokehouse rafter all those weeks.
I can hear his awful screaming
for his trusty single twelve gauge
and his cursing long and loud his dog Old Red.

I can see his sombre body
as he entered from his duty.
I can hear his sound of silence
as he sat at lonely supper
with our forks knives all tinkling
and his moody eyes a blinking
brooding in his own still way,
seeking quiet satisfaction, doing penance
        for his action
knowing in his heart forever
he would love that dog Old Red.

--John W. Crawford
Arkadelphia, Arkansas

COMING OUT PARTY

I wish I could catch that young surgeon who goes
jogging each day by my door--
He's really poetry-in-motion,
a cheetah right down to the core.
Sometimes I am tempted to join him,
but I can't muster up that much zip.
Besides I never could catch him,
and I might even fracture a hip.
They say he's a whiz with the ladies,
and there was never really a doubt..
I'm sitting here scheming and thinking;
What is left that needs to come out.

--Eve Braden Hatchett
Memphis, Tennessee

Poems from: *Take Time to Laugh: It's the Music of the
Soul*, Grandmother Earth, 1993.

A LOOK ON THE BRIGHT SIDE

We burned our bridges long
Before the crossings
Overflowed their banks.
Cost enough to urge the killings

Passion flaming in our hearts.
No matter how often rain washed
Down the sidewalks on the streets of our
      city;
We carried water hoses far beyond the fires of
      foreign war or
Greed or malice.
Trimmed with fancy clothing from
Salvation Army discount lines and
Engulfed in breezes of refinery all the days
      from blackest nights
Seem brightly lit, shining with
A polish not conflagration in a furnace;
Stars burning with a mighty
Twinkle led the living on
Through a collage of internal
Combustion motor cars:
Painted metal chariots rolling
Ever in endless numbers,
Numbered countless iron
Wagons parked forever within
A painted asphalt yard.
He and she together wove a fabric of
      glittering
Resolve.
Meeting at a destination paved with love
      and strength,
They laughed at evil until its
Scowl was spirited at length.
Flesh and bones embraced a
Faith more capital than painful,
Ensuring that their destiny

Stayed human in every form.
Were it a world lacking in Grace, then hand
    of man would pen
Something of that yearning
Toward a better ray of knits,
For every humane effort
Is a smiling benevolence.

--Edith Guy
Memphis, Tennessee

AMNESTIC ATHEISM

For forever
I could have lain there
naked upon the rock --
head resting
cradled in an igneous lap.
Wearing the heat
of the sun alone
my heart
and the rock melted
molding one memory.
Ear to her belly I remember nothing
but faint recollection
of the story she told--
déjà vu of fiery conception
then volcanic perfection

of the rock
where I could sit close to God
and the river --
where I could cleanse my wounds.

Worldly journey
having induced amnesia
the rock was forgotten
and the river
filled with heaven's tears
shed for me stranded
between earth and home
left me unable to recall
where I came from
or to where I would return.

--Martha Cowell Calloway
Franklin, North Carolina

"BEAUTY AND THE BEAST"

Picture this life-size in living color:
Hills and trees stand proudly 'round to screen
A deep ravine with soft, green lining
And a crystal brook meandering through
That's making tinkling music to augment

91

the trilling, thrilling songs of woodland birds.
Who's the artist?   Byline Mother Nature.
Plants burst forth in beauty riotous,
With force and energy to struggle for
Their place in Mother's landscape masterpiece.

"Renew yourselves: a day in the country!"
Is the invitation they broadcast.
"Forget the old routine, that gritty grind.
Come bathe in beauty, pamper every sense:
Of hearing, sight, taste, feeling, smell,
Come live it up with us, Good People."

Mother stands amidst her landscape
Smiling fondly at her human children--
Till they toss around their beer cans,
Burn the vegetation with their bonfires,
Slash and smash the noble trees,
Stash their trash wherever they please,
Pollute the brook with plastic diapers,
Take potshots at the birds who come
To donate music for the beauty fest.

"What ever happened to Ecology--
Or even plain old human dignity!"
Good Mother Earth demands indignantly.

--Ray C. Davis
Mexico

GREEN -- GO   RED -- STOP

The light is green, the way is clear,
Indicated is full speed ahead --
No dread of a time machine to endure,
No rules and regulations to revere.

His mother didn't say be home by one,
Because his mother was already dead,
Overdose supplied by her best friend.
So, who intended that he be a paragon.

His motorcycle he'd christened Comrade Red,
The only friend he could prize, or count on.
Bars offered him a place to anaesthesize,
Speed was the high he sometimes used instead.

He'd run through the light, the officer said,
Crashed broadside into a racing car.
Holding the lifeless body his father wept,
At sixteen, the lights hardest to see are red.

> --Sara Briar Kurtz
> La Canada Flintridge, California

AFTER THE "WILDING"

A villanelle for the Central Park Jogger--April 20, 1989

A spark went out in Central Park last night,
One soul who faced life unafraid--
She fought the Darkness, striving for the Light.

In One mad moment, beyond hope of flight,
She was captured by the wilding horde--
A spark went out in Central Park last night.

She pled with hoodlums to excuse her plight,
Hoping monsters could have pity on a maid;
She fought the Darkness, striving for the Light.

But God turned his head, and shut his sight;
Even her Guardian Angel fled--
A spark went out in Central Park last night.

Some Samaritans found the wounded sprite;
Family, friends, physicians wept and prayed--
She fought the Darkness, striving for the Light.

May she be healed, to work again for Right;
May blind Justice see her tormentors repaid.
A spark went out in Central Park last night--
She fought the Darkness, striving for the Light.

--D. Beecher Smith, II

REVELATION

I know that a gentle age will come.
        In spite of what the warlords say;
Those who endure will not stay dumb.

Though I do not know where from,
        Nor exactly on what day,
I know that a gentle age will come.

Brutality brings death to brutes, but some
        It killed, lived in the peaceful way;
Those who endure will not stay dumb.

Above the noise of the fife and drum,
        Beyond the notes of the march they play;
I know a gentle age will come.

From the dread missiles and the atom bomb;
        Protect and spare us, dear God, I pray;
Those who endure will not stay dumb.

Though this world end at the hands of some.
        Who would not trust in the peaceful way,
I know that a gentle age will come,
Those who endure will not stay dumb.

                    --Beecher Smith, II

DEBBIE'S WHITE CHRISTMAS

The gift of hurt
keeps on giving:
Your last kindness
Consumed our Christmas Club account
Along with my whole week's wages.

At the hospital,
Where the expert medical staff
Repaired my face and your wrists,
They had nothing on hand
To mend hearts.

The emergency room specialist
Would not say that your alcohol
Was more powerful than his alcohol;
He had no drugs
To counteract yours;
No feeling to fill the void of unfeeling
Caused from feeling too much,
Then forcing you
To dull that pain
With more substances.

As the intruding carolers
Inflicted "The First Noel" on families
Stranded in the Waiting room,
I brought the car around
To pick you up
and drive us back

Through the snow flakes,
Wondering
What home have we to return to
So long as you seek solace
In white powder and amber liquids?

--D. Beecher Smith, II
Memphis, Tennessee

All three poems appeared in The *Visitation of Dioysius;*
The last two also appeared in *Generations--Zapisdat World
Anthology*

THE MURHOOING SANDS
To Ann Carlson

That poor folks might grow rich again,
    Beside the Great Lake's shore
They built a town in Michigan
    And named it Singapore.
When all the distant trees were downed,
    They cut the near ones too.
Then they could only sit around
    And watch the sands murhoo!

"My Papa come from Russia's shore;
    My Mama come from Greece;
They take us all to Singapore
    So we can live in peace.
Then when the family is fed
    And all our work is through,

The whole night long we lie in bed
        And hear the sands' murhoo."

But all who'd thought the sands were fun,
        And like the sounds they make,
Soon recognized that what they'd done
        Had proved a grave mistake:
For neither birds nor human song,
        Dogs' bark nor cattle's moo
Could ever have been heard for long
        Above the sands' murhoo.

Why does chaos proliferate?
        As every kind and caste
Aspires to reproduce its state,
        I understand at last!
The birds and mammals copulate,
        Fishes and Reptiles too;
The flowering plants all pollinate --
        But sands -- the sands murhoo!

So ends the tale I've set to song.
        So oft repeated, hence:
No place for man survives for long
        Without the trees' defense;
However great a town may be --
        Tashkent or Timbuktu --
The final sounds of victory
        Will be the sands' murhoo!

                           --Vassar W. Smith
                           Palo Alto, California
From: *The Oven Bird Chorus*

RECYCLED RESPECT

For years they thought we knew it all,
for they were short
and we were tall.
And we used words they hadn't heard,
and met their needs as each occurred:
We answered *whys* and *hows* and *whens*
and helped them make amends with friends.

As years went by, our wisdom waned:
we answered *whys*, and they complained.
They pushed to have the final word
and liked us to be seen, not heard.
No longer did we know it all,
for we were short
and they were tall.

For years they thought they knew it all,
but now they come around or call
to ask us *what*, or *why*, or *how*,
for they're like us--
they're parents now.

--Babs Bell Hajdusiewicz
Katy, Texas

TERRA EXTREMIS

I am the earth--the mother of all life
Past, present, and which may yet come
to stir within my bowels of salted oceans
And shores bemountained hiding paradise
For humanoid and doubt-primordial slime.
           I love you all and hate you all alike!
For millions of years you now have eked existence
Sucking my juices of ascending flavors
And growing bones with muscle to withstand
Ever increasing size of working brain
And skill of tools for bashing chomping slayers.
           I feed you all and starve you all alike!
Your growing skills and nimble-fingered powers
Of using me and every gnarled club
With burning shaft and boiling pot to follow
Into the mouth of cleverest of hunters,
Calling himself the king of hill and beasts.
           I rule over you all and punish all alike!
In ever-growing numbers on whole planet
You, thinking creature, have rashly outgrown
All my resources generated by millennia
Under the crust, in atmosphere and brine below;
You want it all, right now, and only for yourself.
           I give it all and take from all alike!
I groan under your masses and pollution of toxic waste
and excrement in flumes,
Of chemistry organic, bombs atomic,
And ozone layer punctured by your fumes--
Engulfing orb in green-house suffocation.
           I seed you all and choke you all alike!
I will not tolerate this reckless de-evolution
Of forced extinction by self-wanton gods,
Whose slash-burning of jungle for quick profit
And hasty economics for mouth-gnashing

Ensure demise for species on the spot.
                    I give you life and cull you all alike!
Oh, I am not merely kind or cruel--
I harvest-feast on your created hell--
You have intelligence to gormandize your choice!
I give you forth; and then take you back;
I've killed; I kill; and I will kill again!
What will survive? Man, bug, or rock?
                    I am the earth! To me you're all alike!
                              --George V. Mylton
                              Boise, Idaho

THE OLD MAN AND THE EARTH
Gladys Scaife

This is my home, this is my land.
Walk in my shoes and you'll understand,
Why I don't envy your wealth or worth,
My wealth is the wonder of this wonderful earth.

    The old man sat on timeworn doorsteps, hearing
all the strange sounds of the evening, waiting for the sun
to hurry on down. As he waited, he watched his
lengthening shadow on the dry and barren ground.
    Soon he heard footfalls of his son; strong hands
touched him, fanned his hot brow, as a drink from a
nearby bucket he gave. Then side by side they sat in
silence, one old warrior and one young brave.
    "Like father, like son," thought the old of the
young. They've changed his clothes, his tongue, and his
habits. Tried to paint him a shade that just won't take.

For beneath the guise beats a Red man's heart, with a will so strong no power can break."

"Soon sleep will come," thought the old one's son. "He'll quiver and jerk as time turns backward; back to years and days gone by." then slowly the old man lifted his head, and gazed long and hard at a smoke-filled sky.

Then spoke the old man to this young son, Benjamin. "Never do I hear the mockingbirds singing, never do I hear a whippoorwill cry. All of our good earth's disappearing, Benjamin, run before I die. Bring me the cool of a tall green mountain, bring me a south wind gently blowing; patches of color from a new day's start. The soft of grass, a blanket of fresh dew, and the quiet of the dark.

"Now run, my son, to your father run, son. Eagle in the sky no longer flying. Eagle like the buffalo is almost gone. Find our good earth and bring me a memory, back to the old one here at home."

So Benjamin ran like his father had run, through cities and race-ways, litter and junk yards, and not one song was in the wind. Everyone laughed at the Indian crying, searching for things that once had been.

He went back to the reservation, back to the land from which he'd journeyed. The old man listened; then was gone. As Benjamin laid to rest his father, distant drums echoed this song.

"Turn around, my son, and make one more run. Go ask the wise men that sleep in Washington, 'Just how much is all of it worth?' Ask 'Where will they find another America--when the people have destroyed our native earth?'

"Speak proud, my son, as your father has done, and challenge these men who boast of wisdom. Tell them charity breeds laziness and poverty. And they've changed and destroyed man's reasons for living; but never will they change these Cherokees."

The old one in this story that was is the grandfather of
Gladys Scaife of Waynesboro, Tennessee. The son is her
father, originally printed in *The Commercial Appeal*
§§§

THE GIFT

The morning tide is going out,
Making promises to return,
Taking with it the silken mist
Of night, leaving seashells clambering
Over one another at the high tide line.
High seas have washed away
The dunes, made forays under houses,
Leaving stairs askew,
A drunken descent to the beach.
Wooden rocking chairs crowd together,
In the corner of a deck,
As if whispering among themselves
About the storms they have endured.
Where waves have swirled and eddied
around the base of a piling,
a group of small fish huddles
In a shallow sandy grave.
No more to be a gleam of silver
Darting through swells;
No chance to meet a natural death
In steely clutch of Osprey's claws;

Once shining scales now dull grey,
They lie drowned in a sea of air.

A flutter of pink gill, then another,
Brings me to my knees. The fish
Weigh in my hands like damp pebbles
After spring rain. Released into
The ebbing tide, they flip and flop
And disappear into the life-giving sea.

--Rebecca Pierre
Oak Island, North Carolina

ABOVE THE ORDINARY

Don't lose the magic, or hope will fly away with
the white doves.
Grab the brass ring --
pull rabbits of faith out of your
tattered top hat.

Mystery never leaves
a Mona Lisa smile,
and there is MUSIC in the word "Hello."

Don't lose the magic, no matter
if everyone in the whole world
hates each other. . .
                        somebody will hear you sing
above the tears.

Levitate yourself above the ordinary...
            skip when you walk
            ride a rainbow
            chase a shadow
            dance with a willow
            drink a cup of moonlight
            believe in unicorns
            pull silk scarves of doubt
            out of your pockets.

Even if
life hands you paper
roses,
pretend they are heaven sent. . .
don't lose the
magic
or the dragons will
eat
            you.

--Eve Braden Hatchett
Memphis, Tennessee

From: *Of Butterflies and Unicorns* by Frances Brinkley
Cowden and Eve Braden Hatchett, fourth edition
published by Grandmother Earth Creations in 1994.

This anthology includes prize-winning poems, and other material submitted by readers. It also contains excerpts from Grandmother Earth publications. In keeping with that policy the editor includes one of her own poems.

MUD-PIE LEGACY

After each summer rain
mud pies lined my childhood window sill.
Janice and I taught Nancy and Linda
how to roll little mud balls
and pick dandelions
to garnish our dishes which we fashioned inside
fruit jar lids
stolen from mother's preserve-making.
Legends name the earth holy--
something that gives birth
something to die for...
When I walked the plowed earth barefooted
with my father--a farmer--
I learned the ritual of fertility
and wondered how many before me
had the power.
Now I make clay pots
line them up for sale
and wonder if those who buy my vessels
know the meaning within.
I teach my grandchildren to mold and shape
remembering how the native Americans
dug their clay

from the Mississippi
and buried the pots
with their loved ones
returning earth to earth.

--Frances Brinkley Cowden
Memphis, Tennessee

From: *View From a Mississippi River Cotton Sack*

§§§

ACKNOWLEDGMENTS

Works from this collection are reprinted from the
following publications:

Grandmother Earth Publications:

Ashes to Oaks by Shirley Rounds Schirz
Grandmother Earth's Healthy and Wise Cookbook
Kinship by Burnette B. Benedict
Living His Dream: A Farm Journal by a City Slicker by
Geraldine K. Crow
Of Butterflies and Unicorns by Frances Brinkley Cowden
and Eve Braden Hatchett

Take Time to Laugh: Its the Music of the Soul
by Eve Braden Hatchett
To Love a Whale
View from a Mississippi River Cotton Sack
by Frances Brinkley Cowden

Other Publications:

The Visitation of Dioysius, *Generations*, and *Oven Bird Chorus*, by Zapisdat Publishing, Palo Alto, CA
The Mothers of Jesus: From Matthew's Genealogy by Elaine Nunnally Davis , Life Press, Germantown TN
Eve's Navel by Rosemary Stephens,
South and West, Fort Smith AR
The Human Voice
South and West
Tennessee Conservationist
Tennessee Voices
New Collage
The Commercial Appeal

SPECIAL THANKS TO:

Photographs by Cornelius Hogenbirk
Typing Assistance by Elaine Davis
Proof-reading by Dr. Rosemary Stephens
and Dr. Malra Treece
Everyone who entered the 1994 Poetry Contest.

INDEX OF TITLES

Above the Ordinary, 104
After the "Wilding," 94
"And They Were Sore Afraid," 60
Amnestic Atheism, 90
Ashes to Oak, 66
Basil: Herb of Romance, 70
"Beauty and the Beast," 91
Bric a Brac, 27
City Flora, 26
Coming Out Party, 88
Continuum, 53
Day of the Dragon, 64
Debbie's White Christmas, 96
Divine Destiny, 79
Do We Choose Our Memory to be Born, 68
Down and Out, 36
Earth Eminence, 44
Earth's Extinction, 12
The F-15, 43
"Florida Cracker," 62
Forked Tongue Heritage, 37
Frosting, 21
Grandmother Earth's Birthday, 23
Gentleman of Promise, 31
Green--Go--Red--Stop, 93
The Gift, 103
Harass, 38
Heirloom,18
Homecoming, Continued, 14
If the Shoe Fits, 47
Images, 22
Infinite Walls, 59
I Remember Papa, 86
It's...Loofahs!, 72
Kinship, 65
The Little Mares, 57
A Look on Bright Side, 88
Love Dancing, 40
A Magical Realism, 45
Maid, 55

Mocking Bird, 74
Mud-Pie Legacy, 106
The Murhooing Sands, 97
My Love is Jack's Beanstalk, 54
Native Preserves, 28
Newspapered Walls, 42
The Old Man and the Earth, 101
On the Walls of Weidman's, 13
Out On a Limb, 35
The Picture, 53
Rain, 85
Rainbow Rain, 49
Recycled Respect, 99
Refreshingly Autumn, 29
The Return of the Bluebirds, 75
Revelation, 95
Reverential Toast, 63
Saida, 15
Song for the Unborn, 20
Song of the Crow, 41
Summit Up, 37
Tamar, 80
Threads, 34
Terra Extremis, 100
The Vigil, 56
The Wall, Washington D. C., 45
The Weaning of Elvira, 19
When I Write, 67
Who Owns the Mountains?, 32
The Wolf's Side of the Story, 25
Working Mother, 58
Youth, 60

§§§

WHAT'S GOING ON IN YOUR NEIGHBORHOOD?

Christine Lundwald, Jackson Tennessee, started a clean-up campaign that ballooned into a community project. You will be hearing from her in our next issue. Other readers are also invited to send articles.

1995 NATIONAL POETRY CONTEST

FIRST:	$250
SECOND:	$150
THIRD:	$100
FOURTH:	$50
FIFTH:	$25

10 Honorable Mention Awards of $10 each

DEADLINE: JULY 31, 1995

1.   ORIGINAL poems--50 line limit.   The entry fee is $10 for the first   THREE POEMS -----$2 for any additional poem. THE $10 ENTRY FEE reserves a copy of GRANDMOTHER EARTH II.

2. Send two copies of each poem entered:

Copy #1-- no identification.

Copy #2--name and address in right corner, category name and number in the left corner.   List any previous publication with signature under poem.

3.   Send 3x5 card with **name, number, address, telephone number,** title of all poems entered, **amount of fees** enclosed. Place publication release statement and signature on back.   Send check made payable to Grandmother Earth.

4.   Previously published poems should indicate permission to reprint. All **prize-winning poems** will be published in GRANDMOTHER EARTH II.   Other poems **may be** selected by the editor, **with the STATED permission of the author.**

5.   No poems will be returned.   Send SASE for winners list.

A $25 Award will be given to the best environmental story in *Grandmother Earth II*.